Poems of Pain and Power

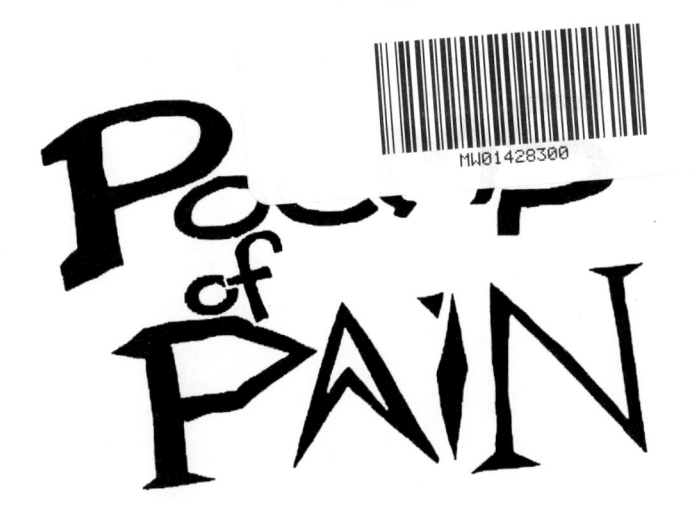

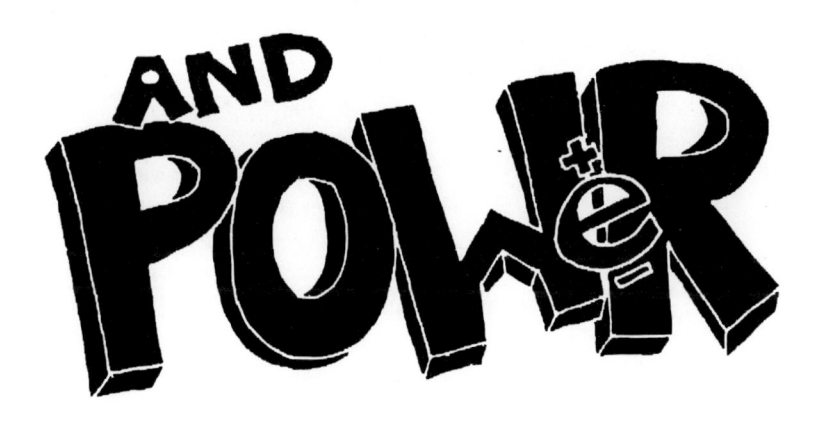

BY SHAKKOI HIBBERT

Poems of Pain & Poetry

Copyright © 2023 by Need Some Koi Inc.
All rights reserved. No part of this publication may be reproduced, distributed or transmitted in any form or by any means, including photocopying, recording, or other electronic or mechanical methods, without the prior written permission of the author, except in the case of promotion for the book/author, or brief quotations embodied in critical reviews and certain other noncommercial uses permitted by copyright law. For permission requests, write to the author, addressed, "Attention: Permission Use", at the email address below:
book@needsomekoi.com

ISBN: 978-1-990728-18-1 (Hardcover)
ISBN: 978-1-990728-17-4 (Paperback)
ISBN: 978-1-990728-16-7 (Ebook)

Cover and Interior Design: What's Your Story - Author Services
Front Cover Graphic Art: Ryan Richard Carr
Author and Back Cover Photo: Kii Moments Photography

"11 faces because of all the faces we wear,
we are still one of one..."

Anti hate and race statement

The author denounces practices of racism, homophobia, transphobia, classism, ableism, ageism, etc. All the words in this book were meant to create love and denounce all forms of hate.

Poetry Catalogue / Table of Contents

FOREWARD

INTRODUCTION

PIECES OF PAIN

- ★ 152 Post
- ★ Experimental Child
- ★ Murder Mirror
- ★ Choosy Veggies
- ★ Grief is Love
- ★ Can't He See
- ★ Stepdad
- ★ Undercover
- ★ Not My Fault
- ★ Unblinded Love
- ★ High School Blues
- ★ Intersectioned
- ★ The Falling
- ★ Love Grave
- ★ New Strangers
- ★ Tires

- ★ Last Year
- ★ Furniture
- ★ The Painment of the Streets
- ★ Leaving Home

PIECES OF POWER

- ★ Reminiscent Rambles
- ★ Message to my Anxiety
- ★ 18 Things
- ★ It's About Me
- ★ Heavy Skin
- ★ The Silence Between the Raindrops
- ★ My Dear Mind
- ★ Generations of Dumbfree
- ★ Mother's Day
- ★ The World is Your Canvas
- ★ Tiger
- ★ November 1st.
- ★ Flying without Wings
- ★ Duality's Your Friend
- ★ Blooming Flowers
- ★ That Feeling
- ★ Love is
- ★ We Rise

- ★ Boom Bap Therapy
- ★ Logged In
- ★ What Gives ?
- ★ To Impose A Black Rose
- ★ B - L - A - C - K
- ★ Slam Poet
- ★ To the Man
- ★ FOMO March
- ★ Rituals
- ★ Shrek
- ★ Hurricane Karen
- ★ Home is Where the Heart IS

BONUS:
- ★ Breaking Barbie
- ★ Body Whispers
- ★ I'm Not Sorry
- ★ Plat Twists
- ★ Hope I never lose you

WRITING PROMPTS
- ★ Perspective Prompts
- ★ Appreciation... Special thank you to...
- ★ Conclusion:
- ★ About the Author

FOREWORD

*P*ieces of pain can be put together to form power. I have always said that poetry has healing abilities, and its duality is described beautifully through Koi's poetry. Through our struggles and the obstacles that are bound to happen in life, we have only two options. One involves the choice of standing after falling and being brave enough to focus on smiling again after donning a frown.

Shakkoi Hibbert is a talented spoken word artist and poet, and has gained credibility in the Toronto/ GTA arts community through her performances, workshops, and commitment to bring culture. Koi is an active artist, who has succeeded in finding her passion–through poetry. As a Poet Laureate who identifies as a visible minority and woman, it warms my heart to see beautiful souls like Koi's thrive in their creativity.

Through poetry I found myself, and books like *Poems of Pain and Power* help me explain this to others. Thank you, Shakkoi, for putting your pieces of pain on display. Through your vulnerability and strength others can witness and learn that they too can turn pain into power.

Murder Mirror – art is a powerful tool, and a pen is often said to be more powerful than a sword. If words have this much power, just imagine the impact that all art forms have on our communities.

Ty the Poetess

Tyneisha Thomas
Barrie's Poet Laureate 2022-2026

Introduction:

Poems of Pain & Power was written to create spaces and places for our not so popular emotions. Art was always in my life, but i didn't realize how it could help heal my life. How can the stroke of a pencil or pen debunk the feelings of anger, grief, and anxiety within me? Then it hit me. It's not only about the art, but the experiences that inspired the art. It's not about how it is performed, but about why it was formed.

Pain is not always a bad thing. If we did not feel pain, we would not know the beauty of overcoming. If we did not know strug-gle, the taste of triumph wouldn't be as sweet. Maybe we go through things to grow through them. I want this book to help you grow through your pain. I want you to practise thinking. I want you to see a problem and start to think and visualise the outcome you want, before the reality you see sets in. I want you to be reminded that you are important, your life matters and that you are not alone. Even though being alone is not a bad thing, once you learn to regulate how you think, you start to gain more power of your own thoughts.

My hope for you, the reader(s), is for at least one poem or reflection question to help you forgive yourself for things that may have happened to you. For things that you didn't deserve to go through, or for what you may be currently going through. Use this book to no longer shy away from the truths of mental pain, but to practice reflecting to turn your pieces of pain to moments of power.

Use the initial questions in the first half of the book to prepare you to read the poem that follows. These questions were added to give the reader a chance to observe the juxtapositions around society, stereotypes and ourselves. I found that asking myself reflective questions, such as, why do I feel pain? How can I feel less pain? or What can I actually do to start to slowly feel better? Helped start to decrease the pain I was feeling. I want readers to know that they can practice the same thing towards their lives. Then use the end notes (found at the back of the book) to Use the "Perspective Prompts", to start, continue or complete your own poem, journal entry or book. You can also use inspiration from this book to start a local poetry club or collective. These are suggestions and not essential to enjoy this book.

Disclaimer *This book speaks of experiences with grief, anger, anxiety, and other topics that may trigger readers. Please seek local resources to promote continued positive mental health practices, if desired. These topics were chosen to help folks feel more comfortable speaking about overcoming pain.*

Pain

Instagram is real... right?

152nd Post

I never wanted you to be my 152nd post.
Maybe in the sense of celebration,
Like a happy birthday story post or a shout out a black king type of post,
But the post I posted was not what I would have thought.
But you can't know what your 152nd post is going to be,
Or if you will make it that far.

It's a game, but it's not.
It's life, no blackjack dealer at the table to guide you in the right right or right wrong direction. Who even cares about a social media post,
But this one I just didn't see it being...152.
Shoot, I could have thought that I would have been your 152nd post...first.

What is a post in real time?
A figment of imagination is my 152nd post just a translation of imaginative frustrations?
What is up with this 152nd post?
152...is it the post that upsets me or the stillness of the post.
Now that I know your body is somewhere still.

A part of all I have now is the pieces of 152, forget you Instagram,
I can't tell if this is rewarding.
I can't tell if 152 is healthy, but right now it helps me.

I guess it's just that as much as I comment under this post,
Even if it were 152 times I couldn't get a solid reply from you.
But I know you would never purposely disrespect me.
You're not ignoring me...
I'm not ignoring ... this.
I guess it's just easier to be mad at this post than at you for being gone.

In my mind I celebrated when I had 150 posts,
I just didn't know two posts later I'd be saying rest in power.

Grief is love.
It has always been love between us and that's why forever it shall continue,
As you surpass the shallow disconnections of connecting with broad media & live forever. Not only as a spirit angel, but a Legend.
Rest in Power Smurf aka DJ Rambo.
Long Live King Rohan.
Psylent Vybz FOREVER.

Every child is a blessing...right?

Experimental Child

Experimental child, experimental child,
Why couldn't there be experimental childs,
Then it wouldn't count if you messed up one cause it was only a trial.
Then maybe I could get in the house with a smile,
Don't care about me just concerned with your pride,
All I need from you is to be a good guide,
Cause forcing things on me just kills my insides.
Alone with you, where can I hide?
Never knew my life would turn into a broken ride,
Secretly, yes I'd love it if we could just talk,
But when you can't see me you begin to stalk,
I have love for you mama, you are my rock.
But what happens when that rock erodes?
Can't get out of your reach, I'm about to explode!
Good communication has long since went cold.
You need to understand everyday I'm getting more old,
And with that means loosen up the control,
And tighten up what we used to hold.
Experimental kid, experimental kid.
Don't act like you don't know what you did.
You say homework is good time well spent.
Not when you drop it down my throat like falling cement.
I don't know if this is what you really meant,

But I hate my life, I'd sell it for free, no rent.
Okay on the face, but in my heart there's a dent.
Going home is like going to jail and every night I am sent.
When can I appeal for my parole?
Eating away at the bits of my soul.
I am sorry I'm not who you want me to be.
I'm the black sheep of the family,
But still I belong to this family tree,
So clear off your glasses so you can finally see,
You can only be you and I can only be me.

Say no to gun violence, because it's a choice...right?

Murder Mirror

When did you change leaders?
When did the streets make you a believer?
The battle of young black boys fighting stereotypes.
But losing and confusing the values of life.
A mother's woes, taken onto your soul.
She gave her baby warm blood for you to make it cold?
I said, she gave her baby warm blood for you to make it cold?
She gave her baby hope and you took away his goals?

Who do you think you are?

Do you think your parents awaited your birth,
So you can grow up and put someone else's in a hearse?

Who do you think you are???

Did you take any needle or pill to protect this child?
Yet you have the AUDACITY to take his breath?
People don't have kids to have...none left.

Who do you think you are?

Oh.. I know, I know.
You have no idea.
You think you are who they told you.
You let the media mould you.
No self love to hold you.
No self love to hold you.

Who do you even console to?
Laundromat life, you fold him, then he folds you.
It's a cycle, but the last spin is not guaranteed.
So listen to the facts I'm about to spin please!

Young black man. You are loved.
You are needed.
The world comes down on you because you can't be defeated.
But only if you KNOW that.
Young black man you are a Prince and a King!
Descendants of Mansa Musa, there is wealth in your blood.
Don't feel rich because you can splurge in the club.
Feel rich because there is Royalty in your blood.
Young black man, old black man, growing black man, gay black man, trans black man, you NEED TO KNOW WHO YOU ARE.
You are worthy, capable, powerful, soft, beautiful, important, Important, IMPORTANT.
But if you are never told so, how could you know??
I'm here to say, STOP THE VIOLENCE.

KNOW YOURSELF,
Because you have more potential than to make a heartbeat silent.

Imperfect means not good...right?

Choosy Veggies

I don't know if I'm writing from a place of lacking love or a place of lacking better choices.

I thought you chose me.
I chose you.

You chose me.
Like I was the brightest looking red pepper at the grocery store.
From the outside I looked the least scarred.

So, you chose me.

Your red pepper... looking so spicy, but you know inside she is sweet.

Maybe there's no path for you.
Not like the paths that are made from the tears running down my face,
No matter what angle I lay.

Have you ever heard your tears fall against your pillowcase?
I want it to be, *Just one of those d a y s...*

Like Monica said,
But it's been a week.

Can I give myself a week to be weak?

Nahhh,
I got things to do.

Sometimes the only comfort found in this comforter.
Thank Jah it absorbs tears too.

See we got that...

Radioactive,

Chemical connections,

Oil and water vibrations,

Toxic communications,

As the clock's tick,

They never waiting.

But I waited to be chosen.
To be that red pepper that was missing from your grocery list.
That red pepper you had to go get, and use on the same day!
As the anticipation for me to arrive has been so great,

You wouldn't DARE to just put me in the fridge and store me away.

I want you to **favor** me.
Not just as some flavour,
But as a nutrient.

An amino essential to your mind, body and soul.
Oh, I want to be a part of your bloodstream.
Turning into vitamin C,
Coming to repair you only when you are cut or feel wounded.
Your internal vitamin C.
That full circle nutrition.

But, that's just the dream of a vegetable.
The dreams of a vegetable.

Choose your veggies wisely.

See unknowingly to me I was like a veggie.

Unaware that I was in the bag of naturally imperfects.

At first a lone red pepper.
Not left, but chosen to be elsewhere.

To be chosen by those who appreciate the value of imperfect vegetables.

A loss is just a loss...right?

Grief is Love

(I was asked to write about something I wish I was told at a younger age, this was my response.)

I wish someone told me about loss sooner.
Like, how it can float like a butterfly, but still sting Muhammud.

See I knew what hardships were.
Those bread, butter and sugar sandwiches.

I was told that just because you are a single mother,
That doesn't mean your kids will be raised without manners and respect.
As if the absence of one parent stuck out like our eyes did when we found out you were sick.

I was told that the real values in life were not from material objects (like the Tamagotchi I raised and lost),
But from the time spent with loved ones.

That saying rang in my head like, *"Jingle Bell, Jingle Bell, Jingle Bell Rock"* during christmas time.

Over and over,
But like trying to dive in the shallow end, the depth for my understanding was not there.

I was told that once I lost certain things, like my hat, scarf, or gloves, they could not be replaced.
I was told to take good care of the things I wanted to keep around me.
I was told about the holidays that **needed** to be sung about.
I was told about the values of going to school in a better country.
I was told to value this country.
This land... once the dreams of my ancestors.

I wish someone told me sooner about the relation to losing a glove vs. losing a person or a parent.

I wish someone told me that even if you value something with all your heart.
Your value or appreciation for it doesn't mean it will always be there when you think you need it.

I wish someone told me that the same way my hand may need that glove,
The glove can be gone.
The glove has served it's time in my life.
I was told about the dangers of losing materialistic things.
Like getting frostbite if I had no gloves.
I wasn't told that you can also feel frostbite in your heart.

And that in this realm loss is dating reality,
And it can be as transparent as the oxygen around us or as oblique and unknown as the bottoms of the ocean.

I wish someone told me to focus on the people I may lose, before I was taught about the things I could lose.

Now that I have had to learn this myself, creating a constant moving monologue.

I know the depths of our connection is centred like the lava under Earth's surface.

I vow to know loss as a distant cousin, and I invite resilience to my family table.

For I vow to have not lost you, but to overstand that I can now praise your existence like the Chlorophyll praises the Sun.
Forever.
As long as I shine, we shine,

Because

Grief is l o v e.

Because emotions are just emotions right?

Can't He See

I hate when so called men use their kids as an excuse,
"Take me back baby I know what I want now I was just confused."
What he says he wants is to help raise his grown youths,
But can't he see at 17 to me he has no use,
He's been a blown fuse,
Damaged unneeded,
So why does this same part of history keep repeating?
Sometimes he complains about how my mom's guy friends have him feel like he's competing,
But when will he see he's already lost the race,
Me believing his silly promises is no longer the case,
Again, another black man who as a father is a disgrace,
Although he has done nothing purposely to indicate,
That he tries to hurt me, he is still a fool and ungreat,
And I feel like he was trying to use me as a tool,
But now I have different people on my pedestal,
And that's me and only me,
In the end who else could I be?
Sometimes I picture him younger when he was on corner streets,
Selling drugs with his friends, feeling like a G,
Was he blind? Couldn't he see,

That in the end the only man I'd want would be the complete opposite of he.
I yell, I cuss, I scream at she,
And like Bob Marley only now I see,
She's the only one I truly need,
And for that I love you mommy.

Some people grow up without parents, so anyone with a bonus parent should be thankful... right?

Stepdad

I looked at you as a Leader,
Can't believe you stayed just to leave us,
To me you are dead, but there will be from me no grieving,
You said you'd come back leaving my mom believing,
Hoping and praying that this house is where you'd be staying,
Why couldn't she see that a stray man will always stay straying.
You took over my living room,
She never asked you to pick up a broom,
I always wondered why you didn't want to move into her bedroom,
Like a car you went zoom zoom,
You're a heartless person leaving her the first time with a child in her womb.
Not caring what happened to either of them, what did you assume?
You even spoke of plans for all of us to move,
My mom's kind heart is what you used your lies to soothe,
Made Stella feel like she got back her groove,
But you never came here to help the family improve.
So the next time you speak to her don't ask about me because I'm not thinking of you.

Best friends are forever... right?

Undercover

It's like I don't know who you are anymore,
Feeling like this got my heart feeling sore,
So, I guess it's time to let my feelings pour.
My deepest secrets I let you explore,
I feel like you know me down to the core,
But it's definitely not mutual,
I feel like you put me in a dark cubical,
This friendship has been so beautiful.
And I think how I'm feeling is stupid.
Why do I need to know anything I'm not God not Cupid,
But I think I just really want to be able to defend,
When I hear any rumours about you I deny it automatically believing obviously this didn't happen because I would have known you're my best friend,
But they said it and to the death I argued.
I called you, you didn't answer so I felt soothed,
Because just in case now I had nothing to prove,
You called back and I felt a little nervous,
Started feeding you verses,
Then I finally got to the point,
Did it happen I asked you and the whole time in my head I was hoping you wouldn't disappoint,

But you did.
Not telling me making me feel like some untrustworthy kid.
Now if someone asks me if this and that is true,
I will not know what to do.
How can I defend you?

These next poems were written for my anthropology class...because it's easy to put yourself into someone else's shoes... right?

Not My Fault

Not my fault...*for your unblinded love.*

I love her, I love her a lot.
I only hit her when I get hot,
Every time she comes around she tries to blow up my spot,
So I hit her once to show her I will not.
Deal with her bull crap,
She needs to understand that if she abuses me verbally it will turn into a scrap.
She burns me like an open wound within it is salt,
So me hitting her is just not my fault.
Is it the fault of blinded love??

Unblinded Love

Taking off the blindfold...

So he hit me once I don't know what to do,
A lot of my friends say give him the boot,
But at least he's not cheating he has stayed true.
But most of the time I'll admit I do feel blue,
I feel used,
Confused,
Everything I want he's quick to disapprove,
So how does he expect me to feel like I haven't lost, I lose.
It's definitely time to move.

The school curriculum has mental health in mind ... right ?

High School Blues

Outside of school, I wouldn't greet ya.
Acting like your super natural when you're just a teacha,
Telling me to do this and that like you're a preacha,
Haven't I told you already this class I don't needa,
So stop tryna tell me what to do I'm my own leada,
Was it because you were bullied in high school,
Why you're trynna enforce these silly and stupid rules,
And stop trying to take my phone away from me you think I have it to be cool?
No it's a necessity I use it as a tool.
Don't call me out in front of the class to make me look like a fool.
To me this class is a joke.
This is all a hoax.
We take a thousand notes.
And you know you're only getting paid to sit,
Because whatever you have been trying to teach, I havent learned it.
And it's not like I'm not trynna learn,
Obviously this credit I'm trynna earn.
But all you teachers give us tests, ISUs and homework at the same time!

And you want 110% from each thing like I don't have other things on my mind.
Every single note is a test,
So don't wonder why teenagers react instead of reflect to release stress.

Intersectioned

Intersectionality we need to break it down misinformation leads society to the ground
Miscommunication it's time to change the station
Open the doors for new relations
Layered by society
Lacking our own variety
We can't let our people suffer quietly

Inner conflicts cause social rivalries
Intersection being gay and a girl
One person split up in an unfitting world

Black lives matter why are you offended? But when a racist becomes president he is commended ?
Black lives matter, screaming to be heard!
Remove the word black and Lives Matter is just another term
BLM is not thug behaviour
We need to stop the institutional erasure.

To erase the suffering of a whole group of people.
Proves that we are still very unequal.
We need to talk to change the sequel.
Open your mind allow it to grow.
To learn more about the world you think you know.

According to science it's impossible for your heart to break and continue to beat at the same time ... right? - The next three poems reflect some of the growing pains of love.

The Falling

Soon my heart will be completely covered with dust,
Because as you proved to me no man with my heart I can trust.
I always did feel like your love had been rushed.
In the end something deep within me you crushed.
I took it like a champ being heartbroken and still hushed,
And slowly I no longer yearned for your love,
My feelings of sadness away I brushed,
I finally know the difference between Love and Lust.

Love Grave

I can't say I wait for your calls any longer,
That's because I'm moving on and getting stronger.
I realized that this love game is too much and it I can't conquer.
So for now, I'll just watch and give my two cents like a sponsor,
I barely wet my feet in this love game and still I feel like I was submerged in water,
And thanks to you for any man to have my heart it will be much harder,
I feel like everyday it shuts down a little bit,
This is something that can't be saved with a first aid kit,
You got me angry like a fire that was lit.
Easy to burn, like a tissue.
But I outed that because I always promised myself I wouldn't deal with my partners issues,
I always tried to tell you exactly how I felt,
But you never knew how to properly respond to me, leaving the problem undealt.
No matter how I felt you made my heart melt.
The melted puddle has now froze,
You sank me down to a new low,
But I've learned to be more alert and never go into anything with my eyes closed.

New Strangers

On him I used to depend,
So how can he ask me to be just friends?
That's something I just can't comprehend,
I could try to but it'd only be pretend,
I kinda wish I'd listened to my heart a long time ago,
I swear my brain told my heart, but it simply replied with, "No".
I could say I wish that we never met,
But I'd hate for you to be my first regret.
I'm not blaming it all on you that would be stupid,
But why did you wait until the end to tell me what the truth is.
Expect the unexpected is my new favorite quote,
I told you not to break my heart and still you left it broke,
Now a little time to blame me,
I shouldn't have showed you my insecurities,
I should have said more sorry's.
After all this though please don't worry, you'll always have a place in my memory's chamber,
To my first love, do be a stranger.

There's a reason for every new season...right?

Tires

You feel like all season tires, during a blizzard.

Keeping me slipping and sliding.
No clear paths in sight.
Just tracks of other crashes.
I gotta get home.
Can't afford the tire change,
So I learn to tread lightly.
Hoping the ice won't notice the lack of grip within my rotations.
I'm spinning,
I'm spinning.
I'm in neural, so they push me.
I push back then realise I'm low on gas.
When did I get into this car?
Should I wait for a season change or should I internally change the season?

Last year reflections > New year resolutions ... right?

Last Year

Last year was the last year..
That I wished for it to be my last year.

Last year, past tears tore through me.
A wrecking ball on a quiet night.
Not sure about our human rights,
Last year.

In the year of last,
I couldn't shake my past.
I put bricks on my path,
Now I'm putting bricks in my bags.

This year.
This was the first year,
I became thirstier than a newborn.
Fussing for just a taste of liquid life.
Forget having teeth,
When I can digest greatness?

Who is she?

Last year I rebirthed a baby that I didn't even know was me. Inner child say hello to intentional identity.

This year.

Don't break furniture, break the feeling to break something.. right?

Furniture

People leave things broken for so long,
Like when my dresser door broke and I made it a part of my wall.
As long as it was being the door...out of sight.
It was okay to be left broken.
Leaving it to make ugly of beautiful scenes.
Even when I thought my room to be the cleanest.
People leave the broken pieces of their metaphoric dresser of hurt behind the doors of their Consciousness.
Instead of just calling the repair man to fix it.
The only difference is you have to want to.

Sidewalks were made for safer streets...right?

The Painment of the Streets

We went from forest trails to paved roads in the name of evolution.

Paving the very roads we may one day lay under.

These paved streets,
Named Streets...
Church Street.
Church street, but there's more grave sites than praying sites, Church Street.

Just another paved street.
Leading you to another street,
Finding more comfort in this cold stone,
Then your own sheets.

Paved streets, not paved ways.

The game was here before you came.
But still,
You had to seem harder than a rock.

Even when the cracks in the streets should remind us that rocks can break too.

Paved streets holding paved systems.
Projecting paid peace.

Making high rise's in downtowns,
I said they making high rises in a down town.
So we chase the high life without taking in the cold ground.

These paved streets.
Colonized streets.
That used to lead us to school, fun and fights.
Sometimes the only way to get out of a bad night.

These streets.

Even with the street signs,
Street lights,
Street lines,

Crashes still happen.

Is it the streets or the people?
Cause the people are led to the streets,
To better streets that they may never see.
Who knows where the CEO's live?

We don't come from the same paved strip, but we still bleed the same.
May I be blessed to one day die in a bed of flowers.
Since too much of my peoples blood, has run on these dutty paved streets.
Let the blood from my brown skin be absorbed by the brown of the Universe.
I can't stand all these dutty paved streets.

Paved Pain.

Covering the beauty of the universe, which is our birthright.

Forget these streets.
Unless they are to pave the way to *Thugz Mansion*, whether the streets made you have to be one or not.

We will now only look to grow in the mountains.
Where the water flows naturally.

We have to step off all the pavement, painement.
Pain that was meant..

And take a breath... in the grass.

Having a home means having safety...right?

Leaving Home

I want to write about home and how it can have so many shapes, but stand in place.

How it can feel so good to be there... and sometimes so bad.
How you sometimes have to find peace in the walls of broken pieces.

Or like when someone leaves the home and the home starts to act as if it no longer is one.
When did you get a personality?
How did you change shape?
(But stay in place.)
Right in front of my face.

Like it did not help raise you, watched you get your hair braided too & watched your parent not make it...home.

We put a lock on the door,
But you still let Cancer come and live here.. In our home..
Did you not understand the assignment?
The roof is for covering the space and the doors...

The doors are supposed to stay locked until the family or the oldest sibling in the house says it's OK to come in.

Home.

I should have known I couldn't trust you.. I mean you nearly ask for blood just to be rented.
You flood and destroy the bricks that were cemented.

Not only did you house another family before us, I bet you treated them like you had their backs too.

But even after I leave you, you will be filled by another! Even after all of our memories.
So home how could I ever feel at home with you??

Short Pieces ... of pieces.

"P is life"

Pain is power
Poetry is P.
P is all you... need.

"Appreciation pain"

I appreciate you,
Still gotta burn you like a sage.
Guess our fumes were not igniting on the same...page.

"Perfect Dose"

Art is better than you.
I can take doses of art to ease the pain.
Goodbye... medication.

"The Voices"

You act as a friend,
But just twist and bend.
Get better... subconscious.

"Daylight Save Me"

More scandals, than scholars,
More oppression, less dollars.

Less daytime, more nights,
More art when there's less light.

"Things I wish equalled "

A Good job and a good life
A smile and being happy
Winter and frozen time
Richness and health
Understanding others and being understood.
Home ownership and home security
Fillers and feeling fulfilled

Old age and wisdom
Young age and ability
Schooling and education

"Flip the switch"

Fearful	Fearless
Rejected	Respectful
Under the weather	Unbothered
Salty	Smooth
Triggered	Trying again
Rage	Reflections
Angry	Aligning
Tired	Triumph
Empty	Energised
Depleted	Destined

Power

Reminiscent Rambles

Gettin over you through conversations with myself,
I'm self defining the real self help.
They say words cut deep,
But that depth deepens when I stab your words at me,
Over and over again.
Just to remind myself of how I feel around you.
Hopeless romantic,
Don't gotta be around you.
Living in my memories,
Like an open cemetery.
Bury me with self forgiveness.
I'm alone and I'm the only witness.
Walking in circles, don't know if I'm going forward or back.
Feelin' like an Urkle to call you back.
But familiar pain is better than new pain.

New strains of underdeveloped people,
I wish I was the next best thing, your Sequel.
Strong minds make the weak feeble.
Pick your poison, choose your evil.
Everyones got an inner DEEVIL,
I mean devil.
My words shake and make your words tremble.
I'm always so remembered,
But I'm bossed in inner lostness.

The costless have no cents.
I'm ranting, but this ain't nonsense.
We going back and forth like Aaliyah.
I don't need to be with ya to feel ya,
But I won't be the one to heal ya.
You can heal and toe to the bottom flo'.

Resiliency making rich of the poor.
Resiliency making rich of the poor.
Take a seed and poh my feelings into it,
Call it a poh-a-tree.

I want you to love me,
The way that I love you on some Ashanti.
That royal love, like the tribes of The Ashanti.
I let Jah Rule and manifest my destiny.
So no bad mind can mess with me.
I like to talk, how I'm feeling,
Because without pain, there is no healing.

True feelings of self devotion.
I'll always be the shea butta... you just lotion.
Dry spells to your Dry cells.
I've been cut...but like a diamond.
That's why my melanin stays shining.
Cut from the Gods.
I am a diamond.
I am a DIAMOND!

Message to my Anxiety

Message to my anxiety,
You secretly inspire me.
Singing loud like a choir's key,
You trynna be the hierarchy.
You focused on me like hocus pocus,
Then I bloom on you, like a lotus.

You're like winter weather and I'm a flower.
With your storming ice and snow you freeze my power.
I'm being blunt to break the ice,
Since you're crawling in my head like lice.
Things are unknown, life's a dice.
Being comfortable costs a price.

I want to be the cashier again,
Fighting you back with the strokes of my pen!
Anxiety if you had a title,
It would be my Least Favourite Idol.
You were built like me,
But you are not like me.
I break free from the walls of anxiety.
Anxiety you are more of a shape shifter,
Than an uplifter.
I see you on road, I see you in pictures.
Moving ice cold to catch your next victim.

Invisible trauma, do you really exist?
Invisible trauma, got me biting my lip.
Invisible trauma, but don't look at her wrists.

Mental metal,
When you can't just think to get better.
All on my throat like a turtle neck sweater.
I'm tired of the self-sabotage.
Anxiety feeling like an inside job.

Anxiety, anxiety,

Not.

Killin' me softly,
But quietly.

Like a twisted spirit guide, inside of me you like to hide.

But today I Have A Message!
Imma look at you like a blessing.
Like you and I equals progression.
Like you and I down the aisle,
But we grocery shopping so I gotta force you to smile.

I won't crush or sit on you,
But imma have to belittle you.

I gotta stay bigger boo.

Think of it as, it's not me it's you.
Think of it as something spiritual.
I was made from the powerful.

Anxiety, anxiety only now I really see.
Anxiety, anxiety you are POWERLESS without me!!
Anxiety I'm the landlord and I'm taking back my key.
I'm moving your butt to the basement.

And don't come back unless you're ready to be complacent.

18 Things

(Message to 18 year old Shakkoi)

1. You will have to watch your mother become physically weak.
2. You will see that strength can evolve from weakness.
3. You will buy a house in a year.
4. You will get into university.
5. You will doubt yourself.
6. You will encourage yourself.
7. You will inspire others.
8. You will not go back to having *Jerri Curls*.
9. You will learn the biggest lessons outside of the classroom.
10. You are Powerful.
11. You will forgive your dad.
12. You will go to Jamaica.
13. You have not lost your touch in writing, you will write again.
14. You will fall in love with a boy... and through that you will fall in love with yourself.
15. You will forgive yourself through forgiving others.
16. You will learn to listen to the universe.
17. You will not let your shyness hinder your destiny to share your words with the world.
18. You do not have to worry, it is already written.

It's About Me

This is not a poem to you,
For you or about you,
Because it's about me.

It's about the times that I did not waste,
Developing myself as you overlooked the shine of my loyalty.

Now look at me, being loyal to me.
As you still cheat on yourself.
I said, now look at me, being loyal to me.
As you still cheat on yourself.

I should have changed my name to gravity the way I held you down.
Now look at me, getting elevated closer to my ancestors so no system can tell me who I am.
No system can force me to agree that the time spent with you was a waste,
Because it was also time spent with me.

You told me I was number one... I said boy I'm no number!
I'm that Thunder, no OKC.
I fed you, no KD.
Everyday of your life I am the MVP.
The one that got away but got deeper within herself.

Now everytime you see me, in your mind you hear *"ah choo"*
Because you can't forget how many times I've blessed you.

My melanin so melanated that I sparkle.
I'm trying to show these young queens, they need to find themselves before a man,
And *especially* before a boy who thinks he can.

Now I'm not against the boy who thought he could there's nothing wrong with dreaming,
But don't claim yourself a King because you figured out how to release semen.
'Cause now I see men,
Wanting to be men,
But they don't believe in themselves.
Two wrongs never make a right.
So to love yourself is an everyday fight.

Now Back to me.
It's about the hindsight that I did not see,
But I won't allow that to mess up my destiny,
Because I still have vision.

And with my vision I can see that not all men are the same.
So I thank the Kings out there who do sustain.
Thank you for believing and achieving love.
Yet another reason I can stand here and say,
My love for you was meant to decay,

But my love for you was never a waste.
It taught me how to love myself more and now I'm free!

And that's why this whole entire poem is still solely...
ABOUT ME.

Heavy Skin

Sometimes I wonder what it would be like to wear skin less heavy.
Like would we get the time for nourishment and not have to grow up before we are ready?

Does God mourn for black skin?
Now how to prove this to my unborn son?

Feeling like we in the matrix with no Keanu.
If Trinity is our lover, I see no holy in it.

I want to have a child that I won't have to worry about mourning.
I want to believe in the good of the morning each time I open my eyes,
But the reality rises so I wish thee a happy one.

Happy rising while we start disguising the hero's we see,
Since they get taken down like posters.

People with pain in holsters,
How do you sleep with hate in your heart?

Allies I'm scared to have a son, cause I don't know if I can save him.
Histories of single motherhood. Is that my destiny?
More reasons to fear for this unborn baby.
I can't erase history, so I grab a pen to write for my future.

Black minds race as we live the races between races.
Races between our blood running on the streets,
Our tears racing each other down our faces.
The race from the media for mental time to breathe.
As we see them, who is us, slain PUBLICALLY!

They say be the change you want to see,
But how can one bring the community to the finish line,
When we see that even in a pandemic that doesn't mean a stop to black crime.

Lemme ask you would you rather Malcolm X or just Malcolm?
Our goal is not take all the problems and just solve em
Legends remind us of the power of self beliefs.
Like they saw what was wrong and used their voices to believe.
Overstand the grand plans to change common beliefs.

Don't carry the weight of our skin on your sleeves.
Don't carry the weight of our skin on your shoulders.
Don't carry the weight of our skin on your hearts.
Might look thin, but it's heavy doe!

Galactic from the spiritual,
Can you hear the beauty of black skin?

Heavy skin,
A tale of alternative perspectives as we praise our heavy skin like the gold that it is weighed in,
MELANIN!!

Reminding us that you are not here to save us,
But to remind us to be united and
That for our rights we have always fighted.
It doesn't matter if we make baby steps,
In the grand scale of things our ancestors saw their escapings as baby steps,
But look at us now!

Look at us now!
Black people hold your head high!
This heavy skin shines light in the darkest times.
Heavy Skin, a quarter to a dime.
Heavy Skin,
Heavy Skin,
I love my MELANIN.

The Silence Between the Raindrops

What if it thunderstorms because our ancestors are reminding us that the sky still opens..?

And that the sky harvests the new day.
Imagine if in each raindrop,
In each raindrop,
There lied the energies of an Ancestor...
Being sent down to harvest the land for a new growth.

Sounds of thunder,
The beauty of the rain.

What if the rain is a reminder to release.
Thunderous sounds,
To express the power of what is above us.

We call it the unknown,
But it knows what it needs to do.
We can't plan for the rain,
An umbrella can't always save you.
But maybe, just maybe you are meant to feel.
I used to run and hide from the screams from the universe,
The THUNDER.
But the sonic waves are not just yelling,
Black people are not just yelling,

We are not just angry,
Thunder is not just angry.
It is moving, we are moving.
We shall release.
I learned to listen in on the silence between raindrops.
I learned to listen in on the _____ between raindrops.

Oh the beauty of the rain.

The tensions that led to the overspill.
The protests from the clouds,
The metaphoric petitions from the air to demand the shedding of water.

The next time you hear the rain or the pain of oppressed people,
Are you listening to what you see, or what you have been told?
The severe weather warnings?
Or do you take the time to listen to the *silence* between the raindrops.

My Dear Mind

I want to,
I swear I do.
I have the choice,
I swear I do.
But when the tempo slows,
And reality is racing around the corner to meet me face to face..

..This mind, so powerful,
takes me off the street and back into the barricading buildings.

Reality... Meet me... next week.
Focus they say, but when silence hits, the binaural beats electrify my veins,
But my mind, my mind sends its own currents to take charge of my journey.
Change my destination, when I'm on my way to peace.
No offence, but Mind, can you handle still reality??
Do you think you are too bold??
Are you afraid to lose yourself in peaceful bliss?

So much on your plate.
Full, but <u>still</u> starving.
Full, but staring at the food.

The food that the chef's still making.
The food that fell off the plate, but still looks up at you with resentful eyes.
Wanting desperately to be back on the plate.

Silence can be your friend if you allow it.
Try it my dear mind,
I beg thee,
Try it, my dear mind.

Generations of Dumbfree

Free-dom of your voice.
We free, but we Dumb.

Free but doomed.
F UR EID...UM,
But we encourage you to practise your religion freeeelyyy.
Freeee..leaders from incarceration.
Freeee..leaders of the government from manipulation.

Freely you came onto this earth,
If you're on the right side of the border.

F-R-E-E, but pay yo taxes F-A-S-T.
D-U-M-B yo voice if it's too loud.
They change your language if it's too proud.
Free to dumb generations,
Leaving generations to fight, to free the dumb of generations.

Dumb is free look at the ads you can see even when you close your eyes.
A free app for a free ad..vertisment,
You do the math.

Dumb is free, so it's mad affordable.
Dumb is free, that's why our phones are soo portable.

Feeling down, but scrolling up.
Free multiplies dumb, that's why education is free.
We gotta subtract the D-U-M-B from the F R E E.
The Babylon is still at ease.
Like giving a homeless man a mansion and saying pay me in blood.
That's the new capitalist way of showing international love.
Free the Muslims in conversion camps.
They MUSE our limbs, until it fits their society's ideologies.
Then MISUSE our kin with no apologies.
Keeping Bi-poc communities in poverty,
The mockercy to call all of this a democracy.
Dumb is free so they giving it out like wifi at McDonalds.
May the free toy in your happy meal not be just another prop for promotion.
Handed down through generations,
Just because it was "free".

Mother's Day

I hate feeling like this is a haunting day,
Because it doesn't really have to be that way,
I had a mom for 19 years, but she couldn't stay,
But that don't mean that all her love has gone away,
You were my role model,
Fresher than a Coke a Cole bottle,
Scratch that, you're still my role model!!
They can take your body, but they can never take your soul.
Our memories together will never grow old.
Some never get to feel a mother's touch,
And I'm not saying 19 years was enough,
But I am blessed to say my mother taught me so much!
Today I had cold feet,
I didn't know this was where my insecurities and fears would meet,
But we came to tell our story,
So you can give your mothers nothing, but love and glory.

The World is Your Canvas

If you zoomed in through a microscope lense,

My DNA would drown your pupils.

My visual biological make up,

Would make your Pineal gland wake up.

My Isle here, but lacking ease.

My paint brush is nothing, but a lit brush...

So I ash it.

Dip it in red and let the fire spread.

Burning the borders and frames of what it's supposed to be.

So I aim for the gold,

But my brush slips into blue.

I send strokes of H_2O,

Trying to use the curve of the rainbow to hold in my canvas.

Keep it looking like a masterpiece.

Since we use depth, shades and colours to master peace.

Tiger

A best friend is someone where when you speak there are no gimmicks.
When my best friend's heart is broken I become a mechanic.
I search for a way to fix it fast I become frantic,
And whoever is responsible for the heartbreak is gonna have it,
Any chance I get to improve her I grab it.
Some spend a lifetime in search of a true friend,
And as of November 5th, 1993, my search came to an end.
I truly believe she was given to me.
My youngest sister she's real family.
I spend every chance I can with her and I haven't regretted a second,
Yes she's younger, but from her I've learned many lessons.
Like how to believe in myself and to stop second guessing.
I couldn't live without her mind, body and soul.
She's always there for me so I never feel alone.
We've been through everything like climbing an epic mountain, starting with small stones.
We crack jokes endlessly as if we were with Kat Williams,
Money I'd spend on her is beyond the billions,
We laugh until we cry,
I couldn't imagine life without her, that would be like a world without the sky,
I'm a bird and she's the wind, which makes us both fly.
Thank God for my sister, Lea-Asha, who is always by my side.

November 1st

L: I can't believe our mom is gone
S: Don't worry baby girl she's where she belongs
L: You know for her we have to be strong
S: The advice she gave never led us wrong.
L: From Monday to Friday working nine to five,
S: She did anything it took to make us survive,
L: Taught us how to fight, taught us how to strive.
S: Always causing laughter whenever she arrived.
L: A mother to many more
S: Not just us four.
L: Our weekend mornings of Dennis Brown
S: She really knew how to flip a frown.
L: Her spirit is here, she'll always be around.
S: Mom had a contagious smile,
L: And a crazy style
S: A mother, lover, provider and giver
L: Truly an angel delivered
S: And now the heavens want her back
L: We can't deny that fact.
S: It's hard to understand, it's hard to believe
L: But we know Sharon Irie, it's your time to be free.

Flying Without Wings

I wanna be
I wanna B like before we added the E,
Just B !

Like before we added IG,
I want to be.

I want to write to make the pages feel felt.
Like how acoustics and acute sounds make hearts melt.

Flying without wings.
Living without the oppression of gravity.
I'm physically here, but mentally thousands of miles away,
new boundaries.
Just to be and see that the only bounds to be broken were that of my insecurities.
Trying to pay off worldly insufficient funds with the wealth of my words.
The bankers are on break, but we're still expected to wait in line.

When was I going to see,
When was I going to see.

I changed my number, it was easier than trying to change my DNA.

When was I going to see.
When was I going to see.
Freedom is within me,
Freedom isn't against me.
Freedom is within me,
Freedom isn't against me.

Duality's your Friend

Over and over there's reminders that it ain't over,

The best of you is constantly being discovered.

Breaking open to recover.
Drop the blanket of need to know
And cover up with the seeds of growth.

Sometimes our tears uncover and release the mental pain of deceit,
From this life, close friends,
Learning to redirect revenge.

Feeling in the dark,
But fiending for the light.
Its alright,
We gon be, Duality shall set you free.

Closing the door of depression,

To see that you're in the mansion of life lessons.

Paying your bills here is a blessing.

When things get tough,
Remember you are enough.

Being down with your demons,
Get up and don't believe them.

Close your eyes, use the voices within.
Treat your inner child like your next of kin.
Greet the bad voices and say good bye.
Say hello to your inner child.

We all fall, but only to create the distance to rise again.
When in doubt, remember that Duality is your friend.

Blooming Flowers

Like watching a flower waiting to bloom,
We do not know what will happen soon,
We watch the flower day in and day out,
We have felt the seed grow stronger and sprout,
But inevitably about the future the mind carries doubt.
One growing flower within a field of fallen flower tales.
Is this developing flower too beautiful to fail?
With fake flowers everywhere will this one prevail?
Rushed production of nature's beautiful flowers could in time turn stale,
This is why true natural beauty takes time.
The creator has never rushed natures production and natures production is divine.
So we must not rush the production of the blooming flower because it is fine.
So away with the worries, away with the force,
And like flowers of nature, let us let nature take its natural course.

That Feeling

You know that feeling, that thing we're all looking for,
That silent yearning beneath the core.
Now I'm no romantic, but that feeling of togetherness,
That feeling of don't ever stress, that feeling of equal happiness.
It's like from the womb we were implanted with the desire to love,
It's a force so not understandable, but yet so international.
You can find this feeling no matter age, sex, or religion.
When you first find love it feels like fates decision.
Two hearts becoming one, a beautiful collision.
Life continues, and things are different,
Eventually that love goes missing',
My hearts beside yours, but it still feels so distant.
When the bond becomes the breaking point,
Then you think, what's the point?
Gave my love and left alone,
My bleeding heart, now resembles stone.
Then I looked up above,
And asked where I could find the GREATEST LOVE,

I looked in the mirror,
And started to see things clearer,
The greatest love is within ME!
If I don't love myself to infinity, how can I expect someone else to?
Positive self-love gives you a new worth.

It got me to a level where I would not allow being hurt.
I learned to not rely on the love of someone else, Because I found so much love in MYSELF!
Now I think of myself and I...I...I get that feeling...
That feeling of togetherness,
That feeling of don't ever stress,
That feeling of equal happiness between me, myself and I !!!!

Love Is...

Love is life. But what they don't tell you is that it is all forms of life. Underlining all forms of emotion, the hidden dosage is love.

When your eyes hold the weight of 2020 right behind its lid's. Pain is present where love can hide. But it is still there. Like the poor tastes of problematic patriotic peasants in the US capitol, affecting the taste buds of Canadian mouths.

Love is the good, the bad, and the ugly.
Love is the judgey.
Love is the prejudice and the racist, for their love for separation unites them.

Love is twisted, Love has never been straight.
We iron the wrong areas of love and burn the very clothes meant to cover us.
We feel hurt in love,
As we feel hurt in the lines made to bound love.

But love is life.
Love is everything.
Love is boundless.
Love is hate.
Because creating space for someone to live in your head, rent free, could never be because you hate them.

You see love is in all places.

Atoms and cells of love all around us bound us in open cages.

Invisible, but felt by the body.
You see love is constant, love is everything.

Love is life.

We Rise

When was the last time you opened your wings underwater,

When was the last time you let your mind be free?

When was the last time you smiled because you didn't have to remember to breathe?

Life gives and takes,
But it's the choices you make,
That give you the power to fly...underwater.

To the Kings, Queens, Extraordinaries,
Femmes, Queers & Non-Binaries,

Now it may feel like you are drowning,
To dive upwards like a rocket,
Into the blue skies of the unknown,
But what is known is that.
Black is beauty, trendsettah, go gettah,
And now we made Mermaids even bettah, even bettah,
Even Bettah! Because we RISE.

Boom Bap Therapy

This is not a rap, it's a Poet-tree with legs.
See I've got to tell my story before she jumps the ledge.
This story started in Tivoli,
Mom from Mandeville,
Father from the Ghetto still,
The beginning, but not the real start.
In Toronto, two beats became one heart.
Two Libras in love in new world situations.
Uhh then came deportation.
Drug dealing parent undercover unaware and,
Drug dealing parent undercover unapparent.
From gold chains to platinum handcuffs
home is hard, but foreign is rough.

I want to be the boom that goes bap,
So I don't bap when the boom comes too soon.

I want to be the boom that goes bap,
So I don't bap when the boom comes too soon.

At the age of eight is when she learned hate,
Called a drug man, but to her just Dad.
Mama trynna make up for the lack of space he take up.
Mama trynna make up for the lack of space he take up.

Mama the black sheep with the queen Armour,
Taught her how to cry less and smile harder.

Dancehall Queen, but a daytime Warrior,
Mess with her four kin??
And you'd be sorry yo!

Stress came in and changed the scenario,
Forecast cancer, forecast dialysis.
No one to uncast her hearts paralysis,
So she cast a pen to stitch her sorrows.
Cause she knows guaranteed is not tomorrow.
House taken, equity calculations.
House taken, equity calculations.
Running for the bag, but you might be racing Satan,
Running for the bag, but you might be chasing Satan.
Shakkoi...Koi gyal, but far from it.
Through the pains and strains she stayed loving.
Rearrange the shame to be discovered.
Suicide was a sewage, I decided to recover,
Suicide was a sewage, I decided to recover.
Never was an angel, but I'm blessed and I'm covered.
Never was an angel, but I'm blessed and I'm covered.
Some say I'm too much, with knowing too little.
I say I'm too much for when I was brittle.
It's simple live the life that you were meant to,
And use art to go BAP before you go BOOM.

I want to be the boom that goes bap,
So I don't bap when the boom comes too soon.

I want to be the boom that goes bap,
So I don't bap when the boom comes too soon

Logged In

I was first logged in for $1.15
It was a little notebook, that was painted green
Finally my own personal inbox,
Somewhere real to keep my deep thoughts,
But what was my username going to be?
Something coool and fly,
You know representative of me.
These letters now represent my personality,
But is that in fact reality?
Because we tweet on Twitter,
But in real life we speak to soul connect.
We use language to make our souls project.
But how can you find who you are if you don't self reflect?
Writing in a notebook and not a tablet changed my intellect.
Click, click, tap, tap I type with my pen.
Click, click, tap, tap the media got you again.
When you can't enjoy a moment without Snap Chattin',
I'm telling you today to SNAP BACK IN.
Social Media can be very influential,
But remember you have the power, you are an artist with a blank stencil.
There's no shame in putting down your phone to grab a pencil.

Find out about yourself, before you are sold a version of yourself. I repeat, find out about yourself, before you are sold a version of yourself.

No matter what you are beautiful, take care of your mental health.
Get natural dopamine from a poem you wrote,
Leave traces of yourself, traces of hope.
Your life has more value than any meme, caption or quote.
So before you take the time to let your social media be nourished,
Make sure you take the time to look within and let your true self flourish!!

What Gives?

I used to wish it was Christmas all the time.
Yes like everyday.
Monday, Tuesday, Wednesday- all of them.
.
Christmas!

I mean imagine waking up to gifts from your most loved ones everyday!

Or Christmas in the Spring?

Imagine Rudolph in a field of Red Roses,

Or Santa sitting in a sauna ?

Or let's imagine more...
Imagine realizing that our loved ones and experiences are the gifts we get each day ?

I remember the last Christmas I celebrated and I was sooo mad,

Hear me out.

I was gifted something from the dollar store !

A basic notebook. The same notebook that became my first published book with now almost 300 copies sold.

What a gift it was for that person to be thinking of me in that dollarstore at that time.
Perspective switch.
I then thought, so what is a real gift?
What is real value?
I had to realize that real gifts can't be scanned.

Like the daily gifts we take for granted.
Like the sun rising to grow our food, materials and more!

But we get mad and go broke to fix up for one day of "gifts"?

I no longer wanted to go broke to feel fixed.

The gift of giving is daily for the living.
Give a smile, a hug some advice.
Sometimes these gifts can save a life.

What is a winter wonderland in a world or wonder ???

The gift is breathing, seeing, believing, hearing and most of all being!!!

Injustice is not knowing the truths of a gift.

Imagine being given breath, but not wanting to live.

What gives??
Not capitalist culture, but life and nature does if you can feel it.

To remind us that giving is a gift of healing.

So much brokenness when we were made whole ?

What gives??
The justice of MEMORIES, THAT LIVE LIKE PEOPLE DO.

This Holiday season don't forget that the gift is YOUUUU.

To Impose a Black Rose

Black, Black, Roses…. In my garden..

My Black is so imposing,
They see it as a warning…

WARNING, the following information may be seen as false, due to our Instagram policy "Hide lines"… I mean Guidelines.

They say Black roses aren't real.
They say that any rose that even comes close is nothing, but an imitation.

A Khardashian Rose.
I know, how could they think we wouldn't notice.

But, I'm supposed to believe Black roses aren't real?

Is a pigeon, not just a black Dove?

Are my black pupils, not just dark brown?

Did Rosa not rise up, by sitting down?

See I say…
The Black rose, erode!

But they told us they never growed.

Maybe Black's rose…where they used to throw stones.

Like when Mary Ann Shadd Cary created the, *Coloured Women's Progressive Franchise Organization,* in the 1800's for Black women to be able to invest in stocks and bonds.

Or when she became the first woman ever, not just a, 'first Black' to own and operate a publishing company.

Speaking of "first Black", they need to add,
First Black… in white history.

Since they tried to deroot us by burning our growing fields,
Robbing us of our lineages.

But the Blacks still rose.

Black women, I mean Black Roses, like Kathleen Kay Livingstone coined the term, "visible minority" and that was in the 1940's.

Not only a leading actress, but a true guide.

Making sure there were scholarships accessible to Black students.

Talk about claiming where the money resides.

Let's talk about another Black Rose.

The Black Rose that birthed me.

The Black Rose that rose from the land of sun, wood and water.

A Jamaican Black Rose, that came to Canada and rose four kids alone.
Worked a 9-5 to keep the home that she owned.

A seed planted so deep that I...
Became a homeowner at the age of 19,
When her petals were put to eternal sleep.

See the Black Roses have been Rose!

We Rose through Parks,
Blacks rose generations,
Blacks continue to raise the Martin's and the Malcolm's.

So when you hear someone say that there is no such thing as a Black Rose...

Ask them who the planter is.

We have to NO our history to YES our future.

I spoke of the Black's that have been Rose, for the culture.

This poem is an ode to all the Black Roses,
That weren't given enough water to grow,
But still pushed through that CONCRETE.

You still grew,
Your legacies pushed through.

I speak of Black Canadian Roses in hopes of one day being considered one, too.

B - L - A - C - K

Bold, beautiful beings. Building beyond boarders. Booed, but barley broken. Booking billions by breaking bad blocks. Buildings break binaries. Blunt bodies body boulders. Best, better, bestest, Black. Basic beings? Ballistic brainstorming. Ballistic brainstorming.

Lacking love, less lust, leaving lost lies. Live long, look levelled. Left liars, lonely leaches lurk. Laugh like, laugh loud. Life laugh, la la la. Lucky locs, lasting lovely. Lucky locs, lasting lovely.

Always attacked although able, although amazing. An apple ages, ageless. Alternative actions against authenticity. Around and alongside all ages. Around and alongside all ages.

Cages corruptly contour courageous conquests. Can't can. Can't Can! Continue cutting capitalist creatures. Created cults, corporations. Curly curls crush criteria. Captain Coco coming. Captain Coco coming.

Kkk, killers. Keeping kids knifed. Keep kicking. Knowledgeable knowing kindhearted Knights. Kunta-Kinte. Kemet kin knowledge kept. Keen Kente Kings & Kweens. Keen Kente Kings & Kweens.

Slam Poet

Slam poet ?
Pshhh,
Not a regular poet lemme tell what I am.
Need some Koi.
Act like you know.
My greatness was inked in a long time ago.

Unseasoned artist...don't even begin.
Like you can't see the flavor oozing from my skin.

I'm the leg that went stank,
I'm a teller, no bank.
The back stretch to your spline.
I'm the freedom to your Quarantine.

I slam in my verse, I make words stand.
My tongue game stings like Will Smith's hand.

Even on a good day I'm the worst.

My lines so heavy they congregate instead of converse.

Before you class me as some poet
Let me show you how I throw it,
And throw up all doubts.

I'm living up to throw down.
I only adjust head to fix my crown.

No showdowns, when I'm too up.
I don't write for trophies because I am one.
If I entered a slam they'd have to change the name and call it a BLAM.

Straight execution when my pen be moving.
Tongue on trigger and we ready for looting.
Slam poet, I can't stand,
Big poet that's the planz, uhhh.
My lines make you duck like I'm dunking in these Stanzas.

I never wrote poetry to win the prize.
I simply write poetry to stay alive.
Slam poet.

To the Man...

To the man that saw me standing alone as if standing alone was the same thing as holding a welcome sign.
I was editing on my phone while you were editing yourself into my personal space.
I'm sorry did you see yourself in the video ?
Oh yes that's right, impossible because I had an earphone in too, hoping to block out the noise of noisy spirits like you.
The Audacity... in this darkness could you not see that my spirit shines light, which like light can burn you.
Come too close and you could get blinded.
Ohh I wish my personal space could be carried like a cage to actually keep me safe.

To the man that followed me to make me cross the street, but I know that's not why the chicken did.
Yet you turned these streets in to a farm as I moved like a chicken to try to reclaim the cracked eggs of my personal space.
I'd rather be a production hen then one sent to the slaughter house. I've heard too many stories of us being attacked, taken without our will, or killed, to apologise for serving you this unwanted conversation chilled.

To the man who didn't have to raise his hand to strike a blow to my embodiment of safe space..

You changed my nights plans, I ran inside, I had planned to walk. I got inside, I tried to laugh, didn't want to seem soft. I opened the door and smiled in the mirror as usual, but it wasn't until I couldn't see myself is when I truly saw myself and finally grabbed my weapon.
I gave up trying to communicate through fight so I gave space for my inner soul to write.

To the man that didn't know that I make lemonade out of lemons this lemon situation just when into the juicer.

To the man that saw me standing alone as if standing alone was the same thing as holding a welcome sign.
If I was holding a sign it would say
Beware, she's got a gun... she's a lyrical shooter.

FOMO March

I am done marching.
For my sanity, desires, dreams or goals.
Marching has put holes in more than just the bottom of my soles.
I'm more of a swaying kind of being.

Floating and flying,
I want to live good and not get caught up in pretending or trying.
I will not have a fear of missing out,
I have fears of not being missed.

What you see and read,
Are the repercussions of the reflective knife I used to cut my head to let my mind bleed.
I always wanted to be a rapper,
But couldn't really wrap things up.
So now I want to be a floater...
Cuz just marching on these broken paths is bond to keep me feeling stuck.

Rituals

Birthday
Church
School
Holidays
Getting paid

Rituals

We shackle up debit, just to stay caged.

Rituals.

Things to keep up with, just to stay paced.

Rituals.

Addicted to rituals but left feeling broke.

Give me a hit of celebration or good family commutation.

They say when you're rich you will,
Calm the individual.

What's the point of being rich with no rituals.

Running shoes with no grip.
Waterfall with no drip.

Getting cut from the family tree,
Creating broken branch remedies.

Meditation is the ritual,
For the individual.

Meditation is the ritual,
For the individual.

Writing, rhyming,
Divine timing.

Dancing, climbing,
Through the darkness shining.

Meditations are the richest ritual for the individual.

Shrek Poem

I'm going to start this acapella.
Fairy tales have come a long way since Cinderella,
You don't always need to be saved by a prince kinda fella,
Ogres are portrayed as bad,
Violent beasts always mad,
Sherk was a tale for new heroes.
Sherk is now a legend like Robert Dinero.
Who said only a prince can save you?
Listen in to the millennial fables,
It's time to bring different hero's to the table.
Fiona was not your typical princess,
She fought off bad guys in a nice dress.
Trapped by a dragon, but she was very smart,
Eating rats too, a perfect Oger counterpart.

Oger's became saviours,
A new type of hero behaviour.
They changed the game with no waivers.
A fairy tale with a spin,
You can be a princess without being thin.
Fiona loved Shrek that was her choice,
Proving to truly be not a damsel in distress, but an Ogre with a voice.

Hurricane Karen

CATEGORY 10!

You move like a bus, but talk like a Benz.
Coming through with your verbal baggage.
Striking down everything in your path.
Hurricane Karen, why are you so mad?
Is it because you are a hurricane?
Just passing by unwanted.

And I, I am the Ocean.
You try to break me.
You shake me, taking me out of my natural form.
Is it because I feed the people and land?
And you, you are just a storm.

Home is where the ♥ is

In my loving spaces, I show up without armour.
I press that record button, as if pushing out a chair to take a seat in my most loving place.

Conversations with you.

No physical space can equate to the weight released when I speak in pieces...
You laminate the puzzle.
In this space, you give me peace back.

This loving space is like a home to me.
Daddy, daughter rearranged by deportation.

We made a new home, connecting foreign lands, through the cell towers that have transformed into lifelines.

My favourite place to go when I'm anxious or sad.

We haven't lived together in years, but you wake me up here.

Those whatsapp good morning memes (even though you say happy rising now),
reminds me that real family love sees no bounds.

Some complain of the strain from these bubbles turned into notes.

Notifications, spoken through vibrations of feeling or sound.

I didn't realise this was a space where you add gems to my Crown.

This loving space where I run in and close the door.
Whispering into the mic, as if we were in the kitchen of this home.
Sharing secrets and the insecurities that no one else sees.

We made this home.
And this poem is a rose as I give you your flowers.
We outsmarted the internet and built an estate of communication.

On the outer webs of our fingertips, a home.
My real homely, loving space.
I love you dad.

Bonus Poems:

Breaking Barbie

You people really messed up.
My anger just transfers to paper,
My paper just turns to more paper..

So why would I use my precious breaths on this beautiful plant to create spells against my vortex.
I am a speaker of life, truth, love and all that is around and in between.
These false prophets trying to box my essence with a mere imitation. LOL
I gave you love, admiration and patience.
You move like evaporation.
All you gave me was baby mama aspirations.

Black bar's be where you find your peace.
Black ball love in a pool full of colours.
I tried to be your Black barbie, but that didn't make you Ken.
I tried to be your only, but you Ushered me into lovers and friends.

These are my confessions,
Imma use you as a lesson.
Like you used me as your blessing.

Imma be the biggest mistake you ever made.
Imma be your top searched page.
You can't block what's on the main stage.

You used your love language to be a savage.
And now I'm Black Barbie with the Badu baggage.

Using my tears to lower the weight of my suitcase heart at the air port of your love.

Unsafe weather warnings, as we fly through the no fly zones.
Looking like a pilot, but moving like a piece of pyrite.
But what's right on a known unsafe flight?
It takes two to tang, so I'll admit to being the O.

Co-dependant co-pilot,
Seeking herbal peace, but choosing verbal violence.
Hearing my truths, but speaking in silence.

Using the razor sharpness of my words to cut through this plastic smile.
A new breath of air...

Breaking my plastic fingers, just to get a grip.

Too many skeletons in my closet to fit these Black Barbie outfits...
When clothless is the only way to cloth them.

What are you wearing ?

She takes off her lashes so she can see,
She takes off her jewels so she can shine,
And she turns off her mind so she can think.

Breaking Barbie..

Body Whispers

If my heart could whisper…it would say you are whole.
Whole like first seeing an A+ on your report card.
Whole like being hugged by rays of Sun after fleeting the cold whispers of air conditioning.
Whole like a working well in the dire daily dryness of an unrisky life…Whole.

If my stomach could whisper it would say.. dinners ready.

Hot seasoned Lentils,
It would remind me that feeling truly full is in fact just a state of mind.
May my dinner be served as disruption.
Chicken to leave me unafraid,
Ground beef to keep my inner dilemmas Grounded.
And some Lamb, so I dare not be Sheep.

My knuckles would thank me for no longer using them to speak to walls. They'd remind me that like me they may seem rock hard, but even a knucklehead can be internally cloud soft.

My ears would thank me for teaching them how to visualize…. and for leaking the conversations between them.

My knees would say, oh gosh!

My feet would remind me that being bare can help bare The soul and that toe size doesn't equal importance.

My feet would whisper that stomping on glass ceilings is also what boots were made for. And that the seasonal walks through depression, were meant to bring me through the peaks and valleys of my mountainous thoughts.

If my lips could talk they would spill the stories of kissing people's hearts and then they would thank you for listening.

If my heart could whisper.

I'm Not Sorry

I have something to proclaim.
I am not sorry and I put that on my name.
I am not sorry for igniting my flame.
I am not sorry for eliminating shame.
I am not sorry for finding ways to alleviate my pain.
I am not sorry for my progression.
I am not sorry about the disconnections.
I've dissed connecting with my destiny to play small in search of empathy.
Just to realise that, that only emptied me.
I'm at the higher self station ready to gas up.
I'm not sorry for going for things that you would have passed up.
As tears run down my face...
I can't be sorry for choosing personal space.

I'm not sorry.

Flat Twists

From the day I was born,
I was scorned with the ideologies already there, about my hair.

As just a baby,
I could not forsee the issues of texture 4c,
Because of the ideologies before me.

Like try to be with someone of a different race to change the make of your baby's hair strands.
And apparently thick, tight curls were not in high demand.

Let me say this for the "preference people".
Saying it will be easier to raise your child because of a hairstyle can seem deceitful.

If you are able to grow hair,
You gotta do something, even if it's just there.

I know everyone has different journeys with their hair and that's fine.
But imma get back to the hair story that's mine.

By the time of grade school, I realised that my hair was different.
My hair "needed to be done", their's didn't.
My natural hair grew towards the sun,

And theirs swayed in the wind for fun.

But then.. I got single braids!
Getting my hair wet without shrinkage was a wave!

But single braids, couldn't save me from feeling singled out.
So by grade five I had Jerri Curls to try to stop all of my baby hairs from falling out.

See the pull of the patterned single braids on my head,
Pretty much left my edges for dead.

From the sounds of crinkle, crinkle to the straight back and single braid jingle,
I entered high school.

I rocked bob's and weaves,
As I bobbed and weaved through my teenage hair bombs.
Then I thought, let's get a perm...why not? It's prom!

I wanted to save money,
So I asked for help from one of my buddies.

This is when I first learned that it can be expensive to be cheap.
I got a perm burn so bad, that it was hard to sleep.
From my right ear to the bottom of my neck,
I suffered from a chemical burn that doctors had to check.

But because it was prom and I didn't want to feel left out,
I put in a leave out to feel like I fit in.

Some wondered why I left graduation at the beginning,
It was because if the wind blew too hard, my cover would be finished.

There were way less BSW's when I was handing in ISU's.
So don't even think about those cute Ankara headwraps from West Africa that we now have access to.

The chemical burn on my head was healing,
I was getting proud of the fact that my hair grew towards the ceiling and then... POW!

The loss of my mama was just a piece of the trauma,
but this is what really digged.

We had to bury her beautiful soul with a wig.

That made me think so differently about the strands on my head.
I no longer cared if they were short, perceived as nappy or too thick.
I just wanted to know that they were mine,
Whenever my soul descends this time.

My thoughts at 19,
Feeling failed and jailed by life.
Paying with art to fill my canteen.

So when I first loced my hair it was to show honor,
To the fact that my mom's locs were cut off, but she didn't call the barber.

We are in a new day and age right?
I loced my hair to make sure my antennas could always feel the light.

Fast forward in life, I cut my locs twice!

No longer locked into the vanity of today's beauty standard insanity.

I freed myself of my locks and the situations that were loced into their fibres.
I wanted to grow higher so I lowered the weights on my head.

Because from the day I was born, I was scorned with the ideologies already there about my hair.

And now because of my texture 4c,
I foresee the beauty within all hair stories.

But... Black hair stories are personal and not to be objected.
Denying someone's skills because of their hair is oppressive.
Refrain from touching, and asking questions.
And whenever you do see Black folks with locs, lace fronts, afros, braids or weave.
It's not just a hairstyle, its a sacred expression of their art, heart and history.
Or maybe just a way that they grieve...

Plat Twists

Hope I never lose you

By the end of this summer I hope to still have something that I once almost lost.

Shoot I almost threw that thing away,

I raised my fist many times to dismiss that thing I thought I could live without.

That thing that released me from doubt.

Hope!

Hope, I'm so sorry I ever doubted you.

I'm sorry about the long summers I spent fighting you,
Gaslighting you.
Telling you that you were not enough,
You're not as valued as money.
You can't buy me anything,
But maybe that's why when we die we can't bring anything..
So before that day let me say,
I apologize to the sparkle in my smile,
The glimmer in my eye.

Hope.

Thinking about being with you makes me feel invincible.

I've historically seen you make mountains move,
While stopping Shaton dead in its track.

How could I have doubted you when you make me feel full without food.

Hope.

With the world on our backs,
You became the Galaxy.

So I'll Sun any piece of doubt pointed straight at me.

Hope.

Hope not just something for the summer to make this clear.

Hope, I'm trying to elope, all day, everyday and for years!

Writing Prompts

Perspective Prompts

Pieces of Pain

- **152 Post**

What about when social media feels too real ?

What are some ways we can learn to appreciate real life more than what we see on social media ?

- **Experimental Child**

How can we support a friend having issues with their parents? How can we try to appreciate or forgive our parents?

- **Murder Mirror**

How can we use art to make our communities a safer place ?

How can art be used to break stereotypes?

What is a stereotype that you can overcome?

- **Choosy Veggies**

How can you choose yourself before waiting to be chosen by someone else?

- **Grief is Love**

How can you use art to continue the legacy of someone you love?

- **Can't He See**

(Requires two pieces of paper)

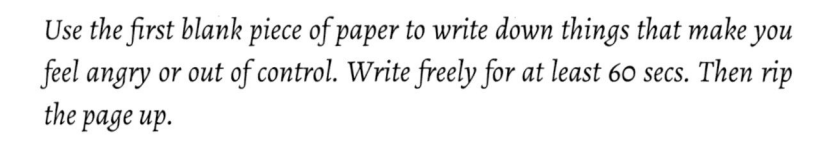

Use the first blank piece of paper to write down things that make you feel angry or out of control. Write freely for at least 60 secs. Then rip the page up.

Use the second piece of paper to write down things that make you feel thankful/happy. Keep this page. Read it often.

- **Stepdad**

What are some potential pros/cons to having a step parent?

How can you learn to communicate better, even when you do not want to?

- **Undercover**

How can you practise treating yourself as a best friend?

- **Not My Fault & Unblinded Love**

What does a healthy relationship look like to you?

- **High School Blues**

How can you use art to relieve stress?

- **The Falling**
- **Love Grave**
- **New Strangers**

According to science it's impossible for your heart to break and continue to beat at the same time ... right ?

- **Tires**

How can the change of seasons sometimes affect you?

- **Last Year**

How can you feel less pressure to be a new person, when the new year comes?

- **Furniture**

How can you use your words to 'break furniture'?

- **The Painment of the Streets**

Describe the last time you got to appreciate nature.

- **Leaving Home**

What does your most loving space look feel, and sound like?

Pieces of Power

- **Reminiscent Rambles**

Write a poem about loving yourself.

- **Msg to my Anxiety**

Write a poem denouncing your fears.

- **18 Things**

Write a poem to your self at the age of five years less than you are now, for example, if you are 17, as your 17-year-old self writing to your 12-year-old self.

- **It's About Me**

Write a poem to make you feel better.

- **Heavy Skin**

Write a poem embracing your culture/nationality.

- **The Silence Between the Raindrops**

Write a poem about a past fear that you have overcome.

- **My Dear Mind**

Write a poem to the quiet parts of your mind.

- **Generations of Dumbfree**

Write a poem about a generation of your choice.

- **Mother's Day**

Write a tribute poem to someone or something.

- **The World is Your Canvas**

Use your words to paint a poem.

- **Tiger**

Write a poem to a family member.

- **November 1st**

Write a poem about a difficult day that you had to overcome.

- **Flying without Wings**

Write a poem to free your thinking.

- **Duality's Your Friend**

Write a poem to the various sides/emotions of yourself.

- **Blooming Flowers**

Write a poem using nature.

- **That Feeling**

Write a poem about yourself.

- **Love is**

Write a poem about love.

- **We Rise**

Write a poem about a fictional character.

- **Boom Bap Therapy**

Write a poem about something that makes you feel inspired.

- **Logged In**

  Write a poem about something that is more important than social media.

- **What Gives?**

  Write a poem about your favourite celebration.

- **To Impose A Black Rose**

  Write a poem about who you know you are.

- **B-L-A-C-K**

  Write a poem using your favourite colour.

- **Slam Poet**

  Write a poem bragging about your favourite art form or sport.

- **To the Man**

Write a poem about feeling safe.

- **FOMO March**

Write a poem about marching away or towards something.

- **Rituals**

Write a poem about rituals you may see.

- **Shrek**

Write a poem based on a movie you like.

- **Hurricane Karen**

Write a poem based on the weather.

- **Home is Where the Heart IS**

Write a poem that speaks from your heart.

Appreciation ...
Special thank you to ...

My Mother, although it broke me to witness you pass away at a young age. I used my pain to want more from this life. It's not over until you think it is. Art has allowed your essence, spirit and love to continue to transform my life. The pain that you went through can never be in vain based off the love it inspired.

To my father, Learoy Hibbert, thank you for thank you for teaching me by showing me. You've taught me to forgive, love and most of all laugh. Even in the Ghettos of Jamaica, you are the rock of our family.

My God Mother Debbie, thank you for reminding me of the juxtaposition of the lion paw. A lions paw is heavy, and sometimes dangerous, but yet the fur is still soft. Thank you for igniting my inner Lioness.

To my big sister, Roxanne Hibbert, thank you for always being a light in my life.

To Aisha Larchie, Merissa S. & Mala D.

Thank you for being there for me when I finally opened my wings...

~Good friends are better than pocket money.~

Conclusion:

I hope these poems and questions inspire you to write. It's not about clout, it's about releasing the doubt that we all sometimes feel. Write, not always to share with others, but to free yourself of all that is on your mind. The motto that helped me continue to push through adversity was to ' Release the Doubt & Step Out '.

After reading this book, how can you release doubts in your life to step out ?

Poems of Pain & Power also has a workbook with more prompts to help folks write. Please visit www.needsomekoi.com to GET YOUR COPIES OF THE WORKBOOK TODAY.

About the Author

When she is not writing poems or promoting Club Koi (Club Kindess On Impact), Shakkoi enjoys spending time in nature, facilitating workshops in poetry or dance and enjoying the small things of life.